Truth and Tradition

Michael John Rood

Print Edition
ISBN: 9798559567259

Copyright © 2020 by Michael John Rood

All rights reserved in accordance with U.S. and International Copyright laws.

No part of this book may be reproduced or utilized in any form or by any means, electronic or mechanical, including but not limited to photocopying, recording, or by any information storage and retrieval system without the prior written permission of the author.

Inquiries should be addressed to:

A Rood Awakening! International
PO Box 1559
Fort Mill, SC 29716
ARoodAwakening.tv

First Edition: November 2020

Traditions.

Traditions can blind us to the truth and cause us to wander in the myopic fog of manmade religious systems for an entire lifetime. Many of the traditions of the Western Gentile Christian Church are merely adapted pagan sun god worship rituals inherited from our ancestors. Centuries ago, believers were forced to compromise with the Roman Emperor Constantine or lose their lives for refusing to bow to his authority. Not only were most of these traditions imported directly from Babylon – there is literally not a single religion practiced upon the face of the earth today that has not been polluted by Nimrod's rebellion against the one true God.

If like me, you came of age in Western civilization, you knew by the time you were three years old that on Christmas Eve, a pot-bellied man in a cherry red suit dropped through the chimney and placed presents under an evergreen tree festooned with gold and silver ornaments. Christian children were told that this was a celebration of the birth of the baby Jesus. And at the time, you were neither intellectually nor philosophically capable of refuting the validity of this tradition. But by the time you entered kindergarten and the debates among your classmates raged, you began to suspect that you had been told a lie. Your concept of reality was shaken, and tears flooded your eyes as you came to the realization that, no, there is no such thing as Santa Claus.

The Hebrew scriptures expose the convoluted traditions of manmade religions and offer an alternative to those who hunger and thirst for truth. Saul, commonly known as the Apostle Paul, wrote that we should not be misled by the traditions and commandments of men, but rely instead upon a tested and proven source of truth, the Torah – the five books of Moses. The children of Israel who camped at Mount Sinai for an entire year received instructions from the Creator through the intercession of Moses. These instructions, called *Torah* in Hebrew, taught us how to govern ourselves and throw off the shackles of manmade religious, political, and economic systems.

Yeshua, or as many know him by his Gentile moniker, Jesus, warned his followers that traditions promulgated by religious leaders are like leaven or yeast, which once mingled with dough cannot be removed. Without the Torah of God, it is thus impossible to separate the traditions of men from the rules of the Almighty.

A rudimentary explanation might be in order here: The English word "tradition" is derived from the Latin *tradere*, which means to lay into the hands of another. When someone lays something into your hands, you expect that the intention of the gift is affirmative. But because traditions can be good or evil, it is the responsibility of the recipient to carefully inspect that which is laid into his hands. After all, Jeremiah said that in the last days, Gentiles would come to Israel and cry out in repentance, "Surely our fathers have inherited lies!" If this is so, what they pass on to us does not magically become the truth by virtue of their sincerity.

All too often, traditions are given to us in innocence and accepted in ignorance; we are indeed like the blind following the blind. Those who are leading us may have no intention to mislead us, but they are blind nevertheless, and we will both certainly fall into a ditch unless we have our eyes opened to the truth.

Unavoidably, this begs the challenging question: What is truth?

Truth means reality — that which *is*. Truth is reality whether one believes it or not. One can believe a lie his entire life, and it will never evolve into truth just to suit his belief system. If we are to live the truth, we must be willing to constantly challenge the traditions and teachings that we've inherited from our parents and religious systems, as well as our own thinking patterns.

I was an adult before I questioned the received images in my mind of Daniel as a young boy standing safely inside the lion's den. Once that picture was embedded, I had no reason to question its validity. But years later, the scriptures offered a new scenario: an aged Daniel, who had been an authority in Babylon under

Nebuchadnezzar, Belshazzar, and eventually Darius, who was deceived into ordering his servant's execution.

Daniel and his Jewish companions, Hananiah, Mishael, and Azariah were raised in Jerusalem and taught the scriptures from the time of their youth. After they were carried away as captives into Babylon, they were renamed Belteshazzar, Shadrach, Meshach, and Abednego, and became eunuchs under the care of master Ashpenaz and were trained for service in the court of the King. Daniel was promoted under King Nebuchadnezzar and was made into an extremely wealthy young man. Daniel's treasure was multiplied twice more during the reigns of Belshazzar and again under Darius the Mede, making Daniel one of the richest men in the kingdom. For more than 60 years, Daniel was in charge of the Chaldeans, an intellectual group of highly trained astronomers, whose numbers included many Judean captives.

Near the end of his life, Daniel was visited by the angel Gabriel and given specific details concerning the arrival of the Messiah, but he was also instructed to seal up some of the information, as it was apparently for him alone to understand and to act upon. Daniel died in Babylon, a eunuch with no heir to whom he could leave his wealth. Yet it would be ludicrous to assume that a man as wealthy and prophetically endowed as Daniel would not have made very careful plans for the distribution of his treasure. After the 70 years of captivity had ended, many of the Jews, especially those in positions of responsibility, stayed behind in Babylon, the most notable being Mordecai and his niece Hadassah, better known as Queen Esther. Daniel would most likely have assigned the execution of his will to his most trusted companions, the Jewish Chaldean astronomers, whom he trained and who remained behind in Babylon.

So, what became of Daniel's estate? It will be nearly 500 years before any hint of Daniel's treasure reappears in the pages of the scriptures. But we must not forget that there is a reason for every word in the scriptures, regardless of how trivial these details may seem to us. With careful exploration of the scriptures and historical records, very compelling pictures will emerge from the text.

****

And speaking of treasure, how many Wise Men came to present gifts to Jesus? Where did they find him? And how was he dressed? Ask any man or woman on the street this question, and the common answer is "three Wise Men found the newborn babe wrapped in swaddling clothes, lying in a manger." Leaving aside the issue that no one today knows exactly what constitutes "swaddling clothes," that is hardly the testimony of the scriptures. We read in the King James version of Matthew's account that an undesignated number of wise men among the Greek Magi came to the house where they found the young child Yeshua living with his mother Miriam and Yoseph. In the gospel of Luke, we read that only the shepherds arrived at the manger.

In any event, blindly calling Christmas the celebration of Yeshua's birth is every bit as questionable as Monty Python's scenario of the wise men entering the wrong house and hailing a child named Brian. Yeshua was actually born on the first day of the Feast of Tabernacles (aka Sukkot), the 15th day of the seventh month on the biblical calendar, which always occurs in autumn, not December 25th when the pagan sun gods were said to have been born. His birth was an intermediate fulfillment of the Feast of Sukkot, or mangers. It is the same word in the Hebrew language. Yoseph was required to live in a sukkah or tabernacle during the entire seven-day feast. Although his pregnant wife Miriam was not required to live in the sukkah, available lodgings in Bethlehem were completely booked, so she was compelled to join her husband on the first day of the Feast of Sukkot and to deliver her first-born son in the sukkah. That is the moment when the word was made flesh and *sukkoted* or tabernacled – or in the King James version, "dwelt among us."

The notion that a lonesome trio laden with treasure crossed the torrid sands of the desert outside the protection of a large armed caravan is simply a non sequitur – they would not have been wise men but rather fools to venture unaccompanied through this wilderness. These Magi, a common term for Chaldean astronomers, were in fact the descendants of the very Jewish astronomers Daniel trained and entrusted with his treasure. Following Daniel's instruction, the astronomers watched the skies for more than 500 years, searching for the great sign in the heavens that finally appeared on the first day of the Hebrew month of Tishri at the end of the fourth millennium – the constellation Bethulah: the virgin clothed with the setting sun, the first sliver of the new moon beneath her feet; and in the 12 stars above her head, the planet Hatsadah; the righteous came into conjunction with the star Habelek, the King in the constellation of Ariel, the Lion of Judah. Thus, on the first day of the month of Tishri on Yom Teruah, the Day of Trumpets, this one-time celestial alignment announced the upcoming birth of the righteous King of Kings, the lion of the tribe of Judah.

Daniel had made provision for the Messiah, and now 500 years later, the executors of his will brought their treasure-laden caravan into the city gates of Jerusalem with the proclamation, "We have come to worship he who is born King of the Jews!" Herod sent them to the neighboring village of Bethlehem, where the prophet Micah said the Messiah would be born. On the very night that Yoseph was commanded in a vision to take the child and his mother and flee into Egypt, the night that Herod's orders to execute all male babies was issued, Daniel's treasure was delivered right to their door. Yoseph himself was so impoverished that he could only afford the poor man's sacrifice of two pigeons at the child's dedication 40 days after his birth, but approximately a year and a half later on the very night they had to escape into Egypt, the provision for their flight in sustenance arrived by special courier. That provision had been made 500 years earlier and prepared for the very moment it was needed.

Truth is always more exciting than fictitious traditions and fairytales based on ignorance of the scriptures. The

Almighty is the master of drama, for when there appears to be no hope, his salvation is revealed. Once we leave our Western Gentile mentality behind as we explore the Bible from a Hebrew perspective, we may experience the paradigm shift of a lifetime.

****

In the book of Ezekiel, the prophet wrote, "The angel brought me to the gate of the house of the Lord, and I beheld women weeping for Tammuz. Then said he unto me, 'Thou shalt see greater abominations,' And he brought me into the inner court, where about 25 men had their back toward the temple, and they faced the east and worshipped the sun." It was in ancient Babylon that sun worship and devotion to Tammuz began. Nimrod built a city that was the center of his world government, within which he was proclaimed to be God. He established a totalitarian rule over his kingdom, reducing men to slaves in his political, economic, and religious system. According to ancient Jewish writings, Nimrod was slain by Noah's son Shem, and his body parts were scattered throughout the land of Shinar.

Nimrod's devoted followers erected a tower that reached into the heavens, a huge obelisk like those we see in Caesarea and in Washington, DC, Heliopolis, Egypt, Rome, London, Paris, and New York City. This phallic symbol is the image of the uncircumcised penis of Nimrod, the father of Babylonian sun god worship, but the Creator calls this an abomination and the image of jealousy. This Roman-created atrocity once discovered in its proper state – toppled over and in pieces – was rebuilt in the summer of 2001. Immediately after its completion during the very month of Tammuz, a Gay Pride parade was held in Tel Aviv, an appropriate inauguration for this obelisk re-erection.

Nimrod's widow Beltis, also known as Semiramis, not willing to let the kingdom slip through her fingers when her husband was killed, proclaimed that Nimrod had ascended into the heavens, that he was now the sun god, and that he had impregnated her with the rays of the sun. Her child was born on the winter solstice on the ancient calendar, December 25th. Forevermore, this day would be celebrated as the day that Nimrod the sun god was reborn as Tammuz.

The little-known birthdate of the Babylonian sun god comes as a surprise to some in the West, but it is common knowledge among Jewish scholars and historians. Israel was taken captive into Babylon for their disobedience concerning sun god worship. They had also been captives in Egypt when they assumed the worship of Ra, the Egyptian sun god, who was born on December 25th. In 168 BC, the Syrian-Greek General Antiochus Epiphanes occupied Jerusalem and set up a statue of Zeus in the temple on Zeus' birthday, and proclaimed that Zeus was God on December 25th. And when Rome conquered Jerusalem, they hung Jewish patriots on the cross of Mithra as a sacrifice to the Roman sun god who was born on – you guessed it – December 25th.

The confusion of languages at the Tower of Babel would scatter the heathen into the far corners of the earth and confuse the names of their gods, but the worship rituals would remain much the same throughout the world. Assuredly, there is one date when Yeshua of Nazareth was not born: December 25th – the birthdate of little baby Tammuz.

According to legend, Tammuz was gored to death by a wild boar in a hunting accident when he was 40 years old. The days of weeping for Tammuz was instituted as one day for each year of his life, in which sun god worshipers would deny themselves a pleasure in this life for the sake of Tammuz' pleasure in the afterlife. When Tammuz' mother died many years later, the exalted queen of heaven was sent back to earth by the gods on the first Sunday after the Vernal Equinox. Nimrod's wife arrived in a giant egg, which landed in the Euphrates River and broke open to allow her to emerge, reincarnated as the bare-breasted goddess of sexual desire, Easter. To proclaim her divinity, Easter changed a bird into an egg-laying rabbit.

In a dingy Hinnom Valley cave, the occult priest would impregnate virgins on the altar of Easter at the Easter sunrise service, and a year later, they sacrificed those three-month old infants on the same altar and dyed Easter eggs in the blood of those sacrificed babies. To this day, one Christian denomination only allows their Easter eggs to be dyed a single, specific color: blood red. They have no idea how the tradition started or what it rehearses, but Easter Sunday is now the day that culminates the 40 days of weeping for Tammuz, called by many Lent. On this day, entire denominations continue a tradition of slaughtering the wild boar that killed Tammuz and eating ham on Easter Sunday – a date when Yeshua most assuredly did not rise from the grave.

Frequently, Easter and Passover are an entire month apart, for the simple reason that they represent the worship of two different gods. Easter is celebrated according to a pagan sun god calendar, but Passover is celebrated according to the observance of the biblical renewed moon and the ripening of the barley in the land of Israel. Yeshua kept the feast of Passover, and all of the rehearsals that were embedded within that feast were fulfilled during the year of his death and resurrection. He was the final Passover sacrifice. His sinless blood paid the price for our redemption.

On the other hand, Easter is a rehearsal of child sacrifice and the fertility rights of pagan sun god worshipers. Which celebration should be kept by today's professed believers? The Holy One instructs us, "Do not learn the way of the heathen and how they worship their gods, and then do the same to me. It is an abomination" (Deuteronomy 12:29-32). Christmas and Easter are not the celebrations of the birth and resurrection of Yeshua of Nazareth, but the timeworn accretions of child sacrifice festivals that originated in Babylon 2000 years before his birth.

We all recognize that the pagan calendar, which has been adopted by the Christian world, names every day of the week and nearly every month of the year after a pagan god or fallen angel, but many are surprised to see that the fourth month on the modern Jewish calendar is named after the pagan god Tammuz in direct violation of the Torah, which proclaims "Thou shalt not allow the names of other gods to come out of your mouth." Like the prophets of Israel, I only reference the names of pagan gods to expose the sick, twisted traditions that we have inherited from our disobedient ancestors. Thanks to them, religious gains have been fabricated by the mind of man that have nothing to do with how God desires to be worshiped. Pop Christian culture adorns itself with the latest hip Jesus apparel and jewelry that ask WWJD – "What would Jesus do?" – but seldom turns to the scriptures to find out.

Yeshua found the place where it was written, said what was written, and did what was written. He did not make up his own theology as he went along. He always obeyed the Torah and said that the Father seeks those who would worship him in spirit and in the truth that was written in stone over 3,400 years ago. When we are ignorant of his instructions, we naturally slip back into

Babylonian sun god worship while we say we are doing it for him. Israel expressed the same ignorance of God's ways when they built a golden calf and said, "Tomorrow is a feast to Yahweh," thus inciting his awesome wrath. Occasionally, I hear the passionate expression, "That is not what Christmas and Easter mean to me!" Perhaps, but the Almighty considers it an abomination to him. Just as he told Abraham in Genesis, he tells those living at the end of the age in the Book of the Revelation, "Come out of Babylon."

At A Rood Awakening! International, we will explore both "testaments" of the Hebrew scriptures from a Hebraic or Jewish perspective. The great commission was to the Jew first, and the Jewish disciples gave their lives to spread the good news of the Messiah to the Gentile world. Here, the Jews will interpret the scriptures that the Jews have written, and ample space will be given to allow the Gentiles to interpret all the scriptures that the Gentiles have written.

And may it all be to the greater glory of YeHoVaH.

ABOUT THE AUTHOR

Michael Rood is an author, historian, teacher, broadcaster, and life-long student of the Bible — a most unique "Biblical Chronologist." Your faith will be renewed as Michael deciphers the parts of Scriptures that have been clouded by misunderstanding, leaving them open to refutation by non-believers and even well-intentioned scholars. Delving deep into the heart of the Scriptures to discover what is expected of us, God's people, Michael illuminates the Bible from cover to cover in a way you've never experienced.

www.ingramcontent.com/pod-product-compliance
Lightning Source LLC
Chambersburg PA
CBHW072147150726
48002CB00004B/1668